BEAUTIFUL MELODIES

FOR VIOLIN DUET

Arranged by Michelle Hynson

ISBN 978-1-70514-204-2

HAL•LEONARD®

Visit Hal Leonard Online at
www.halleonard.com

World headquarters, contact:
Hal Leonard
7777 West Bluemound Road
Milwaukee, WI 53213
Email: info@halleonard.com

In Europe, contact:
Hal Leonard Europe Limited
42 Wigmore Street
Marylebone, London, W1U 2RY
Email: info@halleonardeurope.com

In Australia, contact:
Hal Leonard Australia Pty. Ltd.
4 Lentara Court
Cheltenham, Victoria, 3192 Australia
Email: info@halleonard.com.au

AFTERGLOW

VIOLIN

Words and Music by ED SHEERAN,
DAVID HODGES and FRED GIBSON

ALWAYS

VIOLIN

Words and Music by
IRVING BERLIN

AND I LOVE YOU SO

VIOLIN

Words and Music by
DON McLEAN

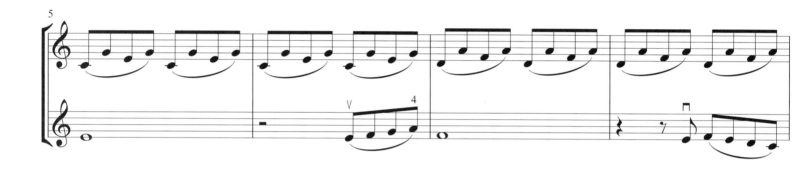

AND SO IT GOES

VIOLIN

Words and Music by
BILLY JOEL

COME AWAY WITH ME

VIOLIN

Words and Music by
NORAH JONES

DON'T KNOW WHY

VIOLIN

Words and Music by
JESSE HARRIS

DREAM A LITTLE DREAM OF ME

VIOLIN

Words by GUS KAHN
Music by WILBUR SCHWANDT
and FABIAN ANDRE

EDELWEISS
from THE SOUND OF MUSIC

VIOLIN

Lyrics by OSCAR HAMMERSTEIN II
Music by RICHARD RODGERS

EXILE

VIOLIN

Words and Music by TAYLOR SWIFT,
WILLIAM BOWERY and JUSTIN VERNON

FAITHFULLY

VIOLIN

Words and Music by
JONATHAN CAIN

HEAVEN

VIOLIN

Words and Music by BRYAN ADAMS
and JIM VALLANCE

I LEFT MY HEART IN SAN FRANCISCO

VIOLIN

Words by DOUGLASS CROSS
Music by GEORGE CORY

I WILL REMEMBER YOU
Theme from THE BROTHERS McMULLEN

VIOLIN

Words and Music by SARAH McLACHLAN,
SEAMUS EGAN and DAVE MERENDA

I'LL BE SEEING YOU

from RIGHT THIS WAY

VIOLIN

Written by IRVING KAHAL
and SAMMY FAIN

LA VIE EN ROSE
(Take Me to Your Heart Again)

VIOLIN

Original French Lyrics by EDITH PIAF
Music by LOUIGUY
English Lyrics by MACK DAVID

LET HER GO

VIOLIN

Words and Music by
MICHAEL DAVID ROSENBERG

LONGER

VIOLIN

Words and Music by
DAN FOGELBERG

Ballad

LULLABYE
(Goodnight, My Angel)

VIOLIN

Words and Music by
BILLY JOEL

MISTY

VIOLIN

Music by
ERROLL GARNER

MORNING HAS BROKEN

VIOLIN

Words by ELEANOR FARJEON
Music by CAT STEVENS

MY FUNNY VALENTINE

from BABES IN ARMS

VIOLIN

Words by LORENZ HART
Music by RICHARD RODGERS

ONLY TIME
from SWEET NOVEMBER

VIOLIN

Words and Music by ENYA,
NICKY RYAN and ROMA RYAN

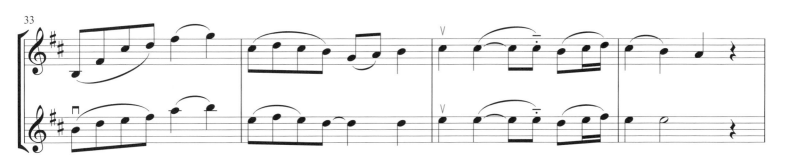

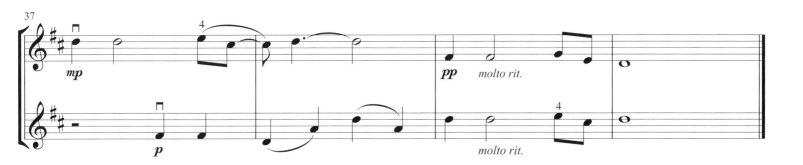

THE RAINBOW CONNECTION

from THE MUPPET MOVIE

VIOLIN

Words and Music by PAUL WILLIAMS
and KENNETH L. ASCHER

SMOKE GETS IN YOUR EYES

from ROBERTA

VIOLIN

Words by OTTO HARBACH
Music by JEROME KERN

SOMEWHERE OUT THERE

from AN AMERICAN TAIL

VIOLIN

Music by BARRY MANN
and JAMES HORNER
Lyric by CYNTHIA WEIL

SONG FROM A SECRET GARDEN

VIOLIN

By ROLF LØVLAND

SWAY
(Quién Será)

VIOLIN

English Words by NORMAN GIMBEL
Spanish Words and Music by PABLO BELTRÁN RUIZ
and LUIS DEMETRIO TRACONIS MOLINA

TILL THERE WAS YOU

from Meredith Willson's THE MUSIC MAN

VIOLIN

By MEREDITH WILLSON

THE WAY YOU LOOK TONIGHT

from SWING TIME

VIOLIN

Words by DOROTHY FIELDS
Music by JEROME KERN

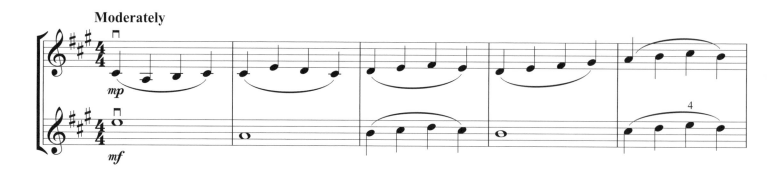

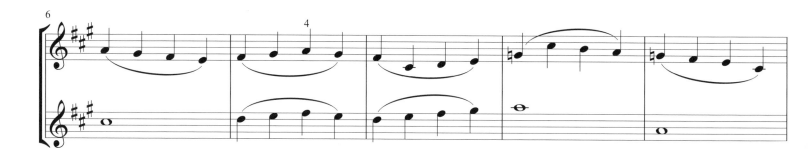

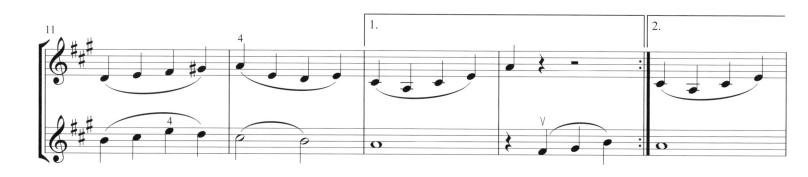

WHERE HAVE ALL THE FLOWERS GONE?

VIOLIN

Words and Music by
PETE SEEGER

Flowingly

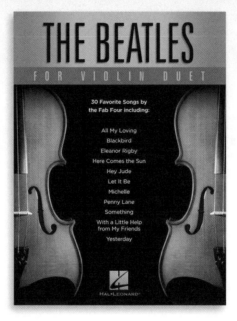